Introduction to
Commercial
REAL ESTATE
LOANS

The *Easy* to Understand Basics

John Crefin

ISBN 978-1-54393-882-1 eBook 978-1-54393-883-8

Printed in the United States of America

Designed by BookBaby
www.Bookbaby.com

First Edition

Crefin, LLC
PO Box 34102
Reno, NV 89533

This book is designed to provide information on the subject of commercial real estate
loans. While the information described in this book is based on experiences, it is sold with
the understanding that neither the author nor the publisher is engaged in rendering legal,
accounting, financial, or other professional services or advice by publishing this book. As
every situation is unique and different, questions and specifics to each situation should be
addressed to an appropriate professional. The author and publisher specifically disclaim
any liability, loss, or risk that is incurred as a result, directly or indirectly, of the use of any
contents of this book.

Now that we have that out of the way, let's move forward!

This book is dedicated to my wife and family. Thank you for the inspiration and encouragement to put my knowledge to paper. Thank you, God, for the guidance, patience, and perseverance—without You, nothing is possible.

Also, though not personally known, thank you to Timothy Ferriss and John C. Maxwell for their inspiring books.

Contents

"Before We Begin"

I am often asked about commercial real estate (CRE) loans or, more accurately, how they work. I often hear:

- "Do I qualify?" "What do I qualify for?"

- "Do you think I can get a loan for [fill in the blank]?"

- "What would the rate be?"

- "What are the fees?"

- "What are the terms?"

- "Is it a good deal?"

These are all good and common questions that are frequently asked. Commercial and residential real estate brokers ask, residential loan officers ask, business owners ask, investors ask, developers, attorneys, accountants, you name it, the list goes on and on. Some are pretty green (rookies with no experience) to the industry and some are seasoned (veterans with experience). But how does it all work? Or more particularly, what does a bank look at? It seems to be unknown territory to most, and I guess to a certain extent it is. But it doesn't have to be. Sure, it takes years and years (and years) to be *really* good at commercial real estate finance ... even decades. But what about the basics?

Before we start, let's be clear, commercial real estate finance is NOT residential real estate finance—there is a *big* difference. The problem with understanding CRE finance is that you either have to be thrown into the lion's den with experience (and hopefully a good mentor) or get your schooling (at least for a basic understanding). The problem with the former is that you don't have the time, opportunity, or desire to dive in to expert status. The problem with the latter is that you spend weeks and weeks (or semesters ... or years) and countless hours going through technical classes (with projects, homework, and various exercises) with much of the material going unused (that is, most don't want to know every detail and all the minutia). Even worse, you spend thousands, literally thousands, of dollars going through this schooling only to retain or wanting to retain the basics.

So what does this book do? This book provides you with a foundation and the basic knowledge of commercial real estate (CRE) finance (i.e., loans). These "basics" are the core to CRE financing. These basics will give you an understanding of this industry, and when you are finished reading you will feel that you have this core knowledge. You will look back, and, one can bet, you will have retained the bulk of it. No need to spend years on it. No need to spend thousands. This book will give you the meat (okay, and *some* side dishes) of CRE finance. It will give you the foundation you are looking for whether you are a real estate broker, lender, investor, business owner, student, or just plain curious. It will give you examples throughout, and as a bonus it will give you a supplement of questions to ask your banker.

Note to readers:

You won't get a lot of fluff to fill the pages of this book, it's actually a pretty thin book if you ask me, which is the point. We are not in it for the hundreds and hundreds (or thousands) of pages. No, we are in it for a quick, easy read packed with content of the basics.

INTRODUCTION

If you haven't already, please read the Preface. Once you have, go ahead and continue (and thank you by the way).

This book will walk you through some of the basics of commercial real estate (CRE) first, and then it will dive into CRE finance. It will walk you through a typical loan structure, the primary drivers of financing, what to expect throughout the loan process, and then on to some other common loan types. It contains examples and footnotes throughout, as well as what I have found to be "Industry Standards." In case you miss any terminology in the footnotes, or simply forget an acronym, the Index/Reference section can be found in Section IV Index/Reference, which will refer you to the page to find the subject matter again. There is also a Supplement you will find useful: a financing questionnaire (questions to ask your lender) at the end of this book. This supplement is a great start to begin the CRE loan process.

Note: The bulk of this book discusses CRE finance when dealing with a typical bank CRE loan, and although things vary from bank to bank, these are pretty normal "standards" on what a lot of banks do. In addition, alternative lenders will undoubtedly be different; however, the basic requirements for them should be more or less the same as you read in this book.

Another note: Pay attention to the footnotes throughout for extra nuggets of information.

I

Commercial Real Estate Overview

Prior to jumping into the actual *financing* of commercial real estate (CRE), we should cover some of the basics of commercial real estate itself. Go ahead and read through this section since the CRE finance section will build off of this section. At the very least, it will be a good refresher for those of you who are already familiar with CRE in general.

1

Property Types

So, what is *commercial real estate* (**CRE**)? It is real estate that is basically not residential real estate, or more particularly, it is not residential housing that contains 1-4 units (1 unit is a single family residence that you or I would use for our home, 2 units = duplex, 3 units = triplex, and 4 units = 4-plex). Any residential property with 5 or more units is considered commercial property (multifamily to be exact), which we will get to shortly[1]. So now that we know what CRE *isn't*, what then, *is* considered CRE? The basic CRE property types are as follows:

- Office

- Retail

- Industrial

---

1 Although the rule of thumb is 5 or more units is considered commercial property and financed as such, 1-4 units also can be financed as a commercial real estate loan; however, this is less common, since the 1-4 units can be financed with traditional residential mortgages (i.e., Fannie Mae or Freddie Mac type loans—although some limitations apply).

- Multifamily

- Other (including mixed use[2], special use[3], etc.)

- Land (primarily for commercial use)

Office

Office properties are just what they seem to be. They are occupied by a business that uses the property for their office, and they typically include service industries. Some examples include: your local real estate office, your friendly insurance agent down the street, your CPA, a call center, a start-up tech company, etc.—you get the idea.

Retail

Retail properties are also pretty straightforward and are what they seem to be. They are occupied by a business that uses the property to sell products or services typically to the public. Some examples include: a supermarket, an electronics store, a clothing store, or a fast-food restaurant.

Industrial

Industrial properties tend to be larger and are typically used by manufacturers and distributors of products. They are occupied by a business that typically sells to other businesses[4]. Some examples include: a mattress manufacturer, an auto manufacturer, a plumbing supply store, a lumber warehouse, or any building that manufactures or stores products or goods.

---

2 See "Other" section later in this chapter.
3 See "Other section later in this chapter.
4 There is another type of industrial building that is called "flex" industrial since it is somewhat flexible. Flex industrial space typically has retail or office space in the front and industrial space in the back. That is, they may sell products or services to the public from a portion of the building (typically the front) and have their traditional industrial space closed to the public (typically the back).

Multifamily

Multifamily properties are residential dwellings and include anything with 2 + units. These properties are occupied by people who use the property as their home. As I mentioned before, to be considered commercial property, a good rule of thumb is any residential property with 5 or more units. Some examples include: a 6-plex (6-unit building), an 8-plex (8-unit building), or that massive 500-unit apartment complex across town.

Other

I only mention this here because there are a variety of unique properties out there that don't fall into the property types already mentioned. Two of the most common "Other" property types are:

- **Mixed Use properties** have a multi-purpose, or mixed use, such as a building with retail stores on the ground floor and multifamily on the 2nd and 3rd floors. Think of places like San Francisco or New York that have retail stores on the bottom floor and apartments above the retail stores.

- **Special Use properties** have a particular purpose, or special use, such as a bowling alley or a gym with a swimming pool.[5]

Land

Land includes raw land (i.e., land with no improvements), finished lots (i.e., land with improvements—including streets, curbs/gutters, water, power,

---

5 Note: Lenders like these properties less than the other property types because the marketability of these are not as good if the loan goes bad. For example, if a bowling alley loan goes bad and the bank has to take it back, it is harder to sell the property than say, a general office space, as a potential purchaser of a bowling alley property would likely have to be another bowling alley operator.

etc., on site), and everything in between[6]. For raw land, think of land that has never really been touched or developed. For finished lots, think of that vacant lot in the middle of the city surrounded by a bunch of buildings.

---

6 After the Great Recession, fewer banks or financial institutions are lending on land. This is due to this property type not having any cash flow. It is just an asset, and banks took a big hit with losses on this property type during the Great Recession. Land and land-related loans actually took some banks down (i.e., caused them to fail). You may, however, find it a bit easier to finance (or quasi finance) land concurrently with a building construction loan. Otherwise, you may have to find private money or hard money that will lend on land, but that comes at a price.

2

Owner Occupied vs. Non-Owner Occupied

Simply put, **Owner Occupied** property is property occupied by the owner. For example, let's say you are a doctor and you buy an office building and move your medical practice into it; this would be an owner occupied property[7].

It is worth mentioning that the definition of owner occupied varies, because an owner of a building can "occupy" a portion of the building and, at the same time, lease out another portion of the building to a 3rd party tenant. A good rule of thumb is if the owner occupies over 50% of the building (based on the building's total square footage), then it is considered owner occupied.

---

7 It is common for owners of buildings to create another legal entity, such as an LLC, to own the building, and then lease the building to their primary "operating" business. For example, Dr. Jones buys a building at 123 Main St., creates 123 Main St. LLC as a legal entity to own the building, and 123 Main St. LLC leases the building to Dr. Jones' medical practice (the operating business). In this instance, it is considered owner occupied because there is common ownership of both the LLC and the medical practice (i.e., Dr. Jones).

Non-Owner Occupied property is the opposite of owner occupied property; it is a property not occupied by the owner. In other words, it is *investor* property occupied by tenants. Following the prior example, let's say you are an investor who buys an office building and you lease it to a 3rd party tenant, such as a doctor; this would be a non-owner occupied property.

3

Lease Types

Leases come in all shapes and sizes, and many come with unique terms and conditions embedded within them (it is amazing what you can find in leases sometimes). Since there are countless variations to leases out there, we will not bore ourselves with thousands of pages of literature and put ourselves to sleep. Instead, we will focus on the 5 main lease types, which are:

- NNN Lease (Triple Net Lease)

- NN Lease (Net Net Lease)

- N Lease (Single Net Lease)

- Full Service Lease (Gross Lease)

- Modified Gross Lease

An **NNN Lease (Triple Net Lease)** is a lease where the tenant (Lessee) pays the landlord (Lessor) a base rent[8] plus additional rent—the additional rent being the cost of the **Common 3 Expenses**, which are: real estate taxes, insurance on the building, and common area maintenance (**CAM**) charges[9]. The tenant also pays for all utilities such as power, water, cable, etc. Most *landlords* prefer this type of lease since it has very few unknowns (unknown expenses and/or increased expenses) because the *tenant* pays for just about everything.

An **NN Lease (Net Net Lease)** is just like a Triple Net Lease; however, 1 of the Common 3 Expenses (real estate taxes, insurance on the building, and CAM charges) is paid by the landlord.

An **N Lease (Single Net Lease)** is just like a Triple Net Lease; however, 2 of the Common 3 Expenses (real estate taxes, insurance on the building, and CAM charges) are paid by the landlord.

A **Full Service Lease (or Gross Lease)** is a lease where the tenant pays the landlord a flat monthly rate of rent. The landlord is responsible for all 3 of the Common 3 Expenses (real estate taxes, insurance on the building, and CAM charges). Most *tenants* prefer this type of lease because this type of lease has very few unknowns (i.e., unknown expenses and/or increased expenses) because the *landlord* pays for just about everything. The tenant may, however, pay for all other expenses such as power, water, cable, internet, etc.

Note: A *true* Full Service Lease includes almost every expense, including the tenant's power, water, cable, internet, etc., which the landlord pays for. However, these so-called true Full Service Leases are pretty rare, and a

---

8 Minimum rent.

9 CAM charges vary but include items such as: janitorial, landscaping, snow removal, security, management fees, general liability insurance, and repairs, among others.

tenant should not count on finding one of these types of leases, nor do landlords typically offer these types of leases[10].

A **Modified Gross Lease** is similar to a Full Service Lease; however, in a Modified Gross Lease the tenant is responsible for additional *future* expenses. Some call this a Triple Net Lease in disguise. The additional future expenses that the tenant is typically responsible for are *increases* in the Common 3 Expenses (real estate taxes, insurance on the property, and CAM charges). In other words, the Modified Gross Lease for the first year (or base year[11]) is a Full Service Lease, but any year after the base year, if any of the Common 3 Expenses (real estate taxes, insurance on the building, and CAM charges) increase, the tenant has to pay for the increased cost. For example, if real estate taxes are $1,000 for the base year and they increase to $1,100 for the second year, the tenant will be responsible for the $100 increase in the second year.

Below is an overview of lease types, which party pays the Common 3 Expenses associated with these lease types, and which property types are generally associated with these lease types.

---

10 More of these true Full Service Leases popped up during the Great Recession since it was a tenant's market (meaning tenants had more power in negotiating lease terms) and landlords did what they could to get tenants (or keep tenants) in their properties.
11 The base year will be defined in the lease, but is typically the first full calendar year after lease commencement, or the first 12 months of the lease.

Lease Type	Expenses Paid by Tenant	Expenses Paid by Landlord	Type of Property Typically Associated with This Lease Type**
NNN	3 of the Common 3*		Retail and Industrial
NN	2 of the Common 3	1 of the Common 3	Retail and Industrial
N	1 of the Common 3	2 of the Common 3	Retail and Industrial
Full Service (or Gross)		3 of the Common 3	Office
Modified Gross	Increases to the Common 3	3 of the Common 3	Office

*Again, the Common 3 expenses are real estate taxes, insurance on the building, and CAM charges.

**The Type of Property Typically Associated with This Lease Type is what is typical in the industry, but they do vary.

Note: Multifamily, although not quoted as a Full Service Lease, really is a Full Service Lease.

Occupancy vs. Vacancy ...
And Then There Is Spec

Occupancy is the percentage of the building occupied (filled, not empty). For example, if you have a 10,000 square foot (SF) building and 8,000 SF of it is occupied, you have 80% occupancy (8,000 SF/10,000 SF = 80%).

Vacancy is the percentage of the building that is vacant (i.e., not occupied, or empty). For example, taking the same 10,000 SF building above, with 8,000 SF occupied, leaves you with 2,000 SF that is vacant. This would give you vacancy of 20% (2,000 SF/10,000 SF = 20%).

Spec (Speculative) is just as it sounds, it is a building that is speculative in nature. Whether this is a to be built building (i.e., construction project), a remodel of a vacant building, or a building with limited occupancy, it is *speculative* in nature because it is uncertain if/when tenants will occupy the building.

Side note: Along with land, speculative development is what got many banks/lenders into trouble during the Great Recession—too many buildings (and houses) were built with no one to fill them.

Tenants/Leases

Tenants (**Lessees**) come in various shapes and sizes, and not all tenants are created equal. Certain types of tenants are just stronger than others. The higher the quality, the more reliable … at least this is usually the case. What this means is that you can rely on payment from certain types of tenants more so than others. Would you rather have a publicly traded 100-year old car manufacturer as a tenant over a start-up? In other words, would you rather have a proven company (that has been around a long time and has strong financials) as your tenant or a start-up restaurant? Who is more likely to honor their lease (and rents) through the lease's entirety? Who is more likely to stay in business throughout the duration of the lease? Which one can you count on more? The proven company is preferred and perceived to be a higher quality tenant.

Side note: A strong, publicly traded company is the type of tenant that is referred to as a **credit tenant**[12].

12 A credit tenant is a tenant that has the size and/or financial strength to be given an investment grade rating by one of the three major credit rating agencies: Fitch, Moody's, or Standard & Poor's.

As with tenants, leases also come in various shapes and sizes, and these too are not created equal. There are a variety of terms included in leases, such as: lease types (previously discussed), lease rates (i.e., rental rates, typically expressed in a per square foot basis), when increases to lease rates kick in (usually annually), whether or not there is a **Tenant Improvement Allowance**[13], whether or not there is a personal guarantee (or a guarantee from an entity)[14], etc. Aside from the lease type and lease rate, the actual lease term, or length of the lease, is the other point of focus.

Common lease terms are typically 3 years, 5 years, 7 years, and 10 years, although leases can range from as little as **month-to-month (MTM)** to as long as 20+ years. In addition to the initial lease term, the tenant usually has an option to extend one or two additional terms. For example, in a 5-year lease, at the end of 5 years, the tenant usually has an option to extend one additional 5-year period (one additional term), or two additional 5-year periods (two additional terms). As a landlord, a longer lease term is typically perceived as better because you won't have to find new tenants as frequently, and thus less chance of vacancy (i.e., less chance of losing rental income).

---

13 Tenant Improvement Allowance (TI Allowance) is an amount (i.e., "allowance") the landlord is willing to spend to renovate the leased space for a tenant. The amount is usually determined during lease negotiations as this cost is usually built into the lease rents over the lease term to reimburse the landlord for their upfront costs.

14 Guarantors will be discussed later in the book (See Chapter 7).

Cap Rates

Cap Rates are essentially the yield (or interest earned) on a given property. Cap rates are usually advertised when a property is listed for sale to let the potential purchaser know how much they will earn if they buy the property. To determine a property's cap rate, you just take the **Net Operating Income** of the property (or **NOI** as it is known ... more on this later in the book) and divide it by the property's sales price. NOI is the net income (**Gross Rents**[15] - Expenses[16] = Net Income, or NOI) of a property *before* paying any loan payments. See Example 1 on the following page for a cap rate calculation.

---

15 Gross Rents include Base Rent and any other rent/reimbursement paid by the tenant. For example, in an NNN lease, Gross Rents = Base Rent + The Common 3 expenses.
16 All expenses related to the property, but typically excludes depreciation, amortization, and interest.

EXAMPLE 1—CAP RATE CALCULATION

Let's say you are looking to purchase a property with the following cash flow and listed sales price:

Gross Rents (Total Rental Income)	$100,000
Expenses	($35,000)
NOI	$65,000
Sales Price of the Property	$812,500
Cap Rate (NOI/Sales Price)	**8%**

In the example above, the cap rate is 8% ($65,000/$812,500 = .08, or 8%); or, alternatively, you would earn 8% on the $812,500 you invested in the property.

II

Commercial Real Estate Loans

Throughout this section, financing will be discussed from the standpoint of typical commercial *bank* financing for a **"portfolio" term loan**[17] since this is the most common (and basic) type of loan. Whether your commercial bank is a large national bank or a community bank down the street, they are all in the same ballpark. Given that markets fluctuate (a bull market, or good times = aggressive bank lending, and a bear market, or not so good times = conservative bank lending), this section will give an overview of a more normalized market (i.e., not a bull market, but not a bear market). Other loan types and financing options will be discussed in Section III.

---

17 A portfolio term loan is a loan held by the bank and is reflected on their balance sheet (i.e., the loan is in the bank's own loan portfolio and typically held until the loan matures or is paid off); in other words, it is not sold to a 3rd party. Note: Some banks out there originate loans and then sell them to a 3rd party, at which point, the bank that originated the loan is not involved anymore. In addition, some banks originate loans, sell them to a 3rd party, and then "service" the loan which makes it appear as though the originating bank still holds the loan on its books as a portfolio loan. Servicing the loan is really just handling a loan (in most respects) on behalf of a 3rd party. For example, a bank that originates and sells a loan to a 3rd party can service the loan for the 3rd party by billing and collecting loan payments from the borrower ... for a fee (paid by the 3rd party).

7

Loan Structure

There are several things, or areas, to consider when looking at a loan and its structure. We will, however, focus on the highlights, which include: borrower(s)/guarantor(s), term, rate, LTV/LTC, fees, prepayment penalty, covenants, and amortization. So without further ado, let's dive in.

Borrower/Guarantor

The **borrower** is the legal entity that "borrows" directly from the bank and typically holds title to the property. There may be more than one borrower on the loan, and, if this is the case, they will be co-borrowers.

Although the borrower can be individuals (i.e., a living breathing person), it is very common for the borrower to be another legal entity.[18] Two very common entities that hold CRE properties (i.e., legally take title of the property) are Limited Liability Companies (LLC) and family trusts. It is

18 Some common legal entities include: a Limited Liability Company (LLC), a family trust, a corporation (S. Corp. or C Corp.), or a partnership. You may want to consult with your attorney and/or CPA to see what would best suit your needs.

also common to form a new LLC for the purpose of holding a single CRE property, which then becomes the borrower (this is due to liability protection, ask your attorney for their legal opinion and what you should do).

A **Guarantor** is a legal entity (or person) that "guarantees" the loan in the event the borrower does not pay or perform on the loan. In other words, the guarantor is on the hook for the loan if the borrower defaults. Often times, there is more than one guarantor on the loan who will guarantee.[19]

Usually, the owners of the legal entity that borrows will guarantee the loan. For example, if the borrower is a newly formed LLC for the purpose of holding a single CRE property, the owners of this newly formed LLC will be the guarantors. Having guarantors on the loan provides additional strength to the loan, or at least another potential repayment source. Perhaps the guarantors have other assets or other income that could support the loan payment if the borrower fails to pay. Banks want to reduce their risk as much as possible and will look to a "warm body" (i.e., a living, breathing person) at the end of the day. So, requiring guarantors is common place and probably should be. If someone (or some entity) is not willing to guarantee a loan, it means they don't want to risk other assets/income that they have, which probably means they have some doubts (or at least some potential concerns) about the property at hand. So, from a bank's perspective, why would a bank believe in the success of the property and repayment of the loan if an owner doesn't?

INDUSTRY STANDARD #1:

Guarantees are usually required on any owner that owns 20% or more of the borrower (or property).

---

19 The bank will typically require that each guarantor provide a guarantee for the full amount of the loan. In other words, if you have a $1,000,000 loan, and there are 2 guarantors, each guarantor will provide a guarantee of $1,000,000 each, not $500,000 each.

EXAMPLE 2—BORROWER/ GUARANTOR STRUCTURE

The following is an example of the borrower/guarantor structure:

Mr. and Mrs. Jones want to buy a property at 123 Main St., so they create 123 Main St. LLC to hold the 123 Main St. property. Mr. and Mrs. Jones also have a family trust (The Jones Family Trust) that will own 100% of 123 Main St. LLC. The Jones Family Trust also has other assets they own and other sources of income as well. The bank would likely structure the loan with 1 borrower and 3 guarantors:

- Borrower: 123 Main St. LLC

- Guarantors: The Jones Family Trust, Mr. Jones, and Mrs. Jones

Although there technically is a difference between a borrower and a guarantor, some would argue that a guarantor really is just a co-borrower at the end of the day.

Term

Commercial real estate (CRE) loans *are not* like a residential mortgage where you get a 30-year term, so don't expect to get one (if you do stumble across one, be prepared to pay a premium for it). You can, however, expect to get a 10-year term (or maybe even a 15-year term). A typical CRE loan is a 10-year loan, **amortized**[20] over 20-25 years, with a **balloon payment**[21] due at the end of year 10. Note: Although it is a 10-year term, it is usually a fixed rate for 5 years with a rate reset at the end of year 5 for the remaining 5 years (you may be able to get a 10-year fixed rate, but the rate will be higher than the 5-year fixed rate, and banks that do offer a 10-year fixed rate often do so via an interest rate swap[22]).

Rate

Again, CRE loans *are not* like a residential mortgage where you get a 30-year fixed rate, so don't expect to get this either (if you do stumble across one of these, be prepared to pay a hefty premium for it as well). You can, however, expect to get a 5-year fixed rate (and in some instances a 10-year fixed rate as mentioned above, albeit at a higher rate). The longer the fixed rate period, the higher the rate will be.

CRE loan rates are typically based on an **index**[23] plus a **spread**[24]. The index varies, but the 3 most common are: the **5 Yr. CMT**[25] (i.e., 5-year Treasury),

---

20 Amortization is essentially the time it would take to pay off a loan given a set loan payment and schedule of when payments are due (more on this later, see "Amortization" section later in this chapter). Banks offer an amortization longer than the term of the loan to reduce the loan payment for the borrower; if banks only offered a 10-year amortization on a 10-year loan, the payment would likely be too steep for most borrowers to handle (or want to handle).

21 Due to the loan term being shorter than the amortization period, there will be a principal balance, in this case, at the end of year 10. As the note matures at the end of year 10, the remaining principal balance is due and referred to as a balloon payment. Note: Although the loan matures at the end of year 10 doesn't mean you can't refinance it with another bank, or the current bank that holds the maturing loan—in fact, it is actually quite common to do so.

22 An interest rate swap is essentially swapping, or trading, a fixed rate for a floating rate with a 3rd party. It is a contractual obligation and you must qualify to even have an option for one. There are numerous types of interest rate swaps, and a lot of books out there on this topic alone, but, for our discussion, these are the basics.

23 An index is a benchmark interest rate. For example, U.S. Treasury rates or the Wall Street Journal Prime Rate.

24 Interest, in addition to, the index rate.

25 The 5 Yr. CMT is the 5 Year Constant Maturity Treasury (aka 5 Yr. TCM, or 5 Year Treasury Constant Maturity). The 5 Yr. CMT is basically just the 5-Year U.S. Treasury rate.

the Wall Street Journal Prime Rate, and the **LIBOR**[26]. The spreads also vary depending on the index used, but each does have a general range—see Industry Standard #2 below—and all 3 are likely to be *similar* rates (at least to start out) at the end of the day regardless of the index and spread used.

Although banks often quote the actual rate for the initial fixed rate period, say 5.25% fixed for the first 5 years, many quote based on an index plus a spread at the time the loan closes. The latter is because it can take many weeks or months to close, and since rates change daily, weekly, and monthly, banks want to ensure they give you the current market rate at the time the loan closes. To figure out your rate (ballpark) on a rate quote based on an index plus a spread, just find out the current rate on the index quoted[27], and add the spread. For example, let's say you were quoted an initial fixed rate equal to the 5 Yr. CMT + 3.5% and the 5 Yr. CMT is currently 1.75%, then your initial rate would be 5.25% (1.75% + 3.5% = 5.25%).

INDUSTRY STANDARD #2:

Loans based on the 5 Yr. CMT generally have a spread of 2.5%-5%, loans based on the WSJ Prime Rate generally have a spread of 1%-3%, and loans based on the LIBOR generally have a spread of 2.5%-5%.

We should also discuss what a **floor rate** (and what a ceiling rate) is. Simply put, a floor rate is the lowest a rate can be. This ensures banks can make a minimum interest rate on the loan they provide. For example, if we use the prior example of the 5 Yr. CMT + 3.5%, the 5 Yr. CMT is currently 1.75%, and there is a floor rate of 5.5%, then the initial rate would *not* be 5.25%

---

26 LIBOR, or London Interbank Offered Rate, is basically the rate that the world's banks charge each other for short term loans. LIBOR rates range from 1 day to 1 year. Note: As of the day this was written, discussions are in process to do away with LIBOR, however this will be done slowly, and not be done until a replacement index is determined. The current front-runner for the replacement of LIBOR is the SOFR (Secured Overnight Financing Rate). 27 You can run a search on these (the 5 Yr. CMT, WSJ Prime, and LIBOR), and numerous sites will pop up with current and historical rates.

(1.75% + 3.5% = 5.25%), it would be 5.5% (the floor rate). Since the floor rate is the lowest the rate can be, you can't get lower than the floor rate.

INDUSTRY STANDARD #3:

Floor rates are generally equal to the initial rate.

The opposite of the floor rate is the **ceiling rate (or rate ceiling)**, or the highest the rate can be. Banks typically don't include a ceiling rate; it is usually just the highest rate legally allowed. Even if you do ask for a ceiling rate, it is usually so high (say 5%-10% over the initial rate) that is doesn't have much impact because rates will likely not get there during the term of the loan. In other words, if your initial rate is 5.25% and the bank agrees to put a ceiling rate on the loan equal to 8% over the initial rate, although possible, it is unlikely that rates will increase that much over a 5-year span (the time when your rate resets), so this ceiling of 13.25% (5.25% initial rate + 8% additional = 13.25% ceiling) is pretty useless (but at least it is a stop gap, or warm and fuzzy for some).

LTV/LTC (Advance Rate)

Loan-to-Value (LTV) is how much the CRE loan amount is relative to the property's value, expressed as a percentage. Simply put, it is the loan amount divided by the *value* of the property[28]. For example, if you have a $750,000 loan amount and a property value of $1,000,000, your LTV = 75% ($750,000/$1,000,000 = 75%).

INDUSTRY STANDARD #4:

The maximum LTV for an OO property = 75%-80%; the maximum LTV for an NOO property = 65%-70%.

---

28 The value of the property as determined by an appraisal.

Loan-to-Cost (LTC) is how much the CRE loan amount is relative to the total cost of a property (i.e., actual cost), expressed as a percentage. This is simply the loan amount divided by the *cost* of the property. For example, you have a $750,000 loan amount and the total cost of the property is $950,000, your LTC = 79% ($750,000/$950,000 = 79%). In a perfect world, the LTV and LTC would be the same; however, this is not always the case. Fluctuations/volatility in CRE markets due to supply and demand, booms, busts, etc., can cause these two ratios to differ substantially.

Banks, like all lenders, usually have a maximum **advance rate**[29] on how much they are willing to lend against a property. Banks will often look at both the LTV and LTC to determine the advance rate. LTC maximums are generally the same as LTV maximums, although some will allow a higher LTC maximum, in the neighborhood of 5%-10% higher (i.e., if the maximum LTV is 75%, the max LTC could be 80%-85%).

Note: Higher advance rates are possible with SBA loans (up to 90% LTV/LTC), which we will touch on later in Chapter 11.

Fees
There are several fees associated with a CRE loan, and below are the most common ones:

- **Loan Fee**—this is the fee paid to the bank (not paid to a 3rd party such as an appraiser, environmental firm, title company, etc.—more on this shortly); the loan fee is typically expressed as a percentage of the loan amount.

---

29 The advance rate is how much the bank is willing to loan against the property, whether it is based on value (i.e., LTV) or cost (i.e., LTC).

INDUSTRY STANDARD #5:

Loan Fees are generally .5%-1% of the loan amount. For example, a 1% loan fee on a $1,000,000 loan = $10,000 ($1,000,000 x .01 = $10,000).

- **Documentation Fee (Doc Fee)**—this fee is also paid to the bank; doc fees are generally $250-$500, but can reach to several thousands of dollars as well.

- **Appraisal Fee**—typically $2,500-$5,000. I know, a little bit of sticker shock when you first hear it, but this is the industry standard. Remember, this is not a residential loan (or residential appraisal). Commercial appraisals are much more in depth and, from my experience, typically 100-200 pages (but can definitely be more or less). Speaking of more or less, if you have a complicated or large transaction, expect the appraisal cost to be substantially higher. Also, you can avoid an appraisal with a loan amount of $500,000 or less (if the bank is willing to do their own internal evaluation), but with anything more than a $500,000 loan, you are on the hook for an appraisal.

- **Environmental Fee**—this can be a bank form environmental questionnaire to fill out, an online environmental report, a Phase I ESA, or more. This basically screens a property for any potential environmental concerns.

  - Bank form environmental questionnaire—typically free. It asks the buyer (and maybe seller) questions and you answer them to the best of your ability and knowledge.

  - Online environmental report—depending on the type and depth it can vary, but typically about $500-$1,000. These reports will search a variety of historical records and data-bases and will conclude with a high risk/low risk evaluation along with a summary of findings.

     o   **Phase I ESA (Phase I Environmental Site Assessment[30])**— typically $2,000-$3,000, but varies by market. This is an analysis by an environmental engineer that actually visits the property as well as searches historical records and databases, and provides a conclusion with a high risk/low risk evaluation along with an opinion of the findings.

     o   While the three methods above are common, the "more" is not as common. The more is basically a **Phase II ESA** or **Phase III ESA** that can get *very* costly. A Phase II is triggered when a Phase I recommends that further investigation of a property is warranted. A Phase II will have the environmental engineer go out to the property/site and do some digging, take soil/water samples, and analyze them to see if further remediation on the property is necessary, or will sign off that everything is okay (in their opinion). A Phase III is triggered when a Phase II recommends it. A Phase III is the remediation and correction of the environmental issues.

INDUSTRY STANDARD #6:

Unless the property is a high risk property profile[31], banks typically do not require Phase I ESA's on loan amounts less than $1,000,000.

---

30 A "Phase One."

31 Properties that have historically had a higher rate of environmental problems/remediation such as gas stations, automotive repair shops, dry cleaners, etc.

- **Title Insurance Fees**—varies based on the amount of **title insurance**[32] and any additional endorsements (i.e., additional insurance coverage) a bank may need/require. Title insurance ensures a bank that it has "clean" title (or at least acceptable title) to a property. Title companies will search public records and other data sources and provide a report (**preliminary title report [prelim]** or title commitment) to banks that lets them know about the property itself. Common items reflected on title reports include: existing liens/loans on the property, **easements**[33] on the property, **CC&Rs**[34], unpaid service fees/taxes on a property (i.e., unpaid sewer fees, garbage fees, real estate taxes, etc.), and other rights to the property (i.e., mineral rights, gas rights, water rights, etc.), among others. Upon a bank's review of the prelim, the title company will provide the title insurance (and endorsement coverage), at the close of the loan, that the bank requires. In addition to title insurance, title companies also charge an **escrow fee** for coordinating/conducting the loan close; escrow fees also vary depending on the loan size, complexity, and work involved. As a rule of thumb, the larger the loan amount, the more title insurance you will need, and the more it will cost. As mentioned above, title insurance and escrow fees vary greatly depending on a variety of factors, but you can plan to pay a couple thousand dollars to start with and go up from there.

- **Other Miscellaneous Fees**—there are countless other fees out there that can be added to the above, some are pretty minor (a

---

32 Banks usually require the minimum amount of title insurance to equal the loan amount or replacement cost of the property.

33 A right of way, or right to enter, or cross, a property.

34 CC&Rs (Covenants, Conditions, and Restrictions) are rules that govern the use, maintenance, look, and a variety of other factors, related to a property or properties. CC&Rs usually govern a common commercial center with multiple buildings. For example, an office park with several buildings is likely to have CC&Rs to govern what the property owners can and cannot do to their property. CC&Rs are generally in place to maintain or enhance the common commercial center.

few dollars), but some are quite large (thousands of dollars). Since it would be impossible to name (and price) them all, the following are some other common fees that you can/will likely encounter: flood certification fee (to verify if the property is in a flood zone or not), legal fees (for documentation preparation and/or review), tax service fee (a service paid to a 3rd party that monitors your property to make sure you pay your real estate taxes), property inspection fees (structural inspections, pest inspections, etc.), and a reserve study fee (a 3rd party report that estimates what capital improvements or maintenance is/will be needed, when they will be needed, and the cost to do them, which the bank may require a cash "reserve" account be set aside to ensure the improvements/repairs can/will be completed), among others.

Note: Remember, the above fees are related to getting the loan in place, it does not include all the ongoing costs related to the property.

Prepayment Penalty

A **Prepayment Penalty** is a penalty you have to pay when you pay the loan off early. Bank loans typically have a prepayment penalty with a term that matches the term of the initial fixed interest rate period. For example, let's say Mr. and Mrs. Jones have a loan with a 10-year term, and the loan has a fixed interest rate for the first 5 years. In this instance, a bank would likely have a 5-year prepayment penalty on this loan. Simple, straight forward prepayment penalties are expressed as a percentage of the outstanding loan balance and nothing more. Note: There are a variety of prepayment penalty types out there (yield maintenance, defeasance, etc.), so beware and understand what you are signing up for; however, when working with banks, the simple, straightforward prepayment penalty is usually what you get. It is industry standard to have a *declining* prepayment penalty, although some have a *flat* prepayment penalty. In our Mr. and Mrs. Jones example, they would probably be offered one of the following:

- Declining 5-year (or 5, 4, 3, 2, 1) prepay—this means that the prepayment penalty would be 5% in year 1, 4% in year 2, 3% in year 3, 2% in year 4, and 1% in year 5 (after the end of year 5, there is no prepayment penalty). For example, if Mr. and Mrs. Jones were in the 3rd year of their loan and wanted to pay it off, they would have a 3% prepayment penalty on their outstanding loan balance at that time. For instance, if their loan balance at the time of pay off was $950,000, their prepayment penalty would be $28,500 ($950,000 X .03 = $28,500).

- Flat 5-year (or 5, 5, 5, 5, 5) prepay—this means that the prepayment penalty would be 5% in year 1, 5% in year 2, 5% in year 3, 5% in year 4, and 5% in year 5 (after the end of year 5, there is no prepayment penalty). For example, if Mr. and Mrs. Jones were in the 3rd year of their loan and wanted to pay it off, they would have a 5% prepayment penalty on their outstanding loan balance at that time. For instance, if their loan balance at the time of pay off was $950,000, their prepayment penalty would be $47,500 ($950,000 X .05 = $47,500).

A couple of notes:

- Just as banks ensure Mr. and Mrs. Jones their 5-year fixed rate, with the prepayment penalty in place, the bank is ensuring, at least to some extent, they will get *some* of their income that they projected to get at the start of the loan, in the event the loan is paid off early.

- Although prepayment penalty terms typically match the initial fixed rate period, it is not always the case. For example, a loan with an initial 5-year fixed rate period may have a 3-year prepayment period (i.e., a declining 5, 3, 1 or 3, 2, 1 prepayment penalty).

Covenants

CRE loans come with a variety of **loan covenants** (conditions or measurements to keep the loan in good standing throughout the term of the loan), the most common of which are the **Debt Service Coverage Ratio (DSCR)** and the LTV requirements.[35]

The **DSCR** (aka **Debt Service Coverage (DSC)** or **Debt Coverage Ratio (DCR)**) covenant is a ratio to measure a property's cash flow; this measurement is usually conducted annually. Banks will usually require financials (tax returns, profit & loss statements, and **rent rolls**[36]) annually to allow them to measure this covenant. In the most simplistic form, it is the property's Net Operating Income divided by the property's **Debt Service Obligations** (loan payments), which can be expressed in the following forms:

- DSCR = NOI/Loan Payments

- DSCR = **EBIDA**[37]/Loan Payments

- DSCR = **EBITDA**[38]/Loan Payments

- EBITDA = Earnings Before Interest, Taxes, Depreciation, and Amortization

Note: All of the above should give you a similar (if not the exact same) DSCR.

---

35 Some other common covenants are: deposit, liquidity, working capital, and debt-to-worth covenants.

36 A rent roll is a breakdown, or list, of tenants of a property, and states each tenant's: unit/suite number, SF they occupy, lease rate (i.e., how much rent they pay), lease commencement, and lease expiration.

37 EBIDA = Earnings Before Interest, Depreciation, and Amortization. In other words, EBIDA is equal to Net Income + Interest + Depreciation + Amortization.

38 EBITDA = Earnings Before Interest, Taxes, Depreciation, and Amortization. In other words, EBITDA is equal to Net Income + Interest + Taxes + Depreciation + Amortization.

INDUSTRY STANDARD #7:

OO properties require a minimum DSCR of 1.20-1.25, and NOO properties require a minimum DSCR of 1.25-1.35.

EXAMPLE 3—DSCR COVENANT CALCULATION

Let's say you have an office property with the following annual cash flow (NOI) and you have a minimum DSCR covenant of 1.35. Further, you have two possible future scenarios (Future Scenario A and Future Scenario B) as shown below.

	Loan Commencement	Future Scenario A	Future Scenario B
Gross Rents	$165,000	$175,000	$155,000
Expenses	($57,750)	($61,250)	($61,250)
NOI	$107,250	$113,750	$93,750
Loan Payments	$78,000	$78,000	$78,000
DSCR	1.38	1.46	1.20

At Loan Commencement, you have a DSCR of 1.38 ($107,250/$78,000 = 1.38).

In Future Scenario A, over the course of a few years, rents and expenses on the property both increase. In this case, your DSCR would be 1.46 ($113,750/$78,000 = 1.46), and you are in compliance with your DSCR covenant as it is greater than the minimum requirement of 1.35.

In Future Scenario B, over the course of a few years, rents decrease and expenses increase. In this case, your DSCR would be 1.20 ($93,750/$78,000 = 1.20), and you are not in compliance with your DSCR covenant since it is less than the minimum requirement of 1.35. In this scenario, a bank may require a loan restructure to right size the loan to bring the DSCR back in compliance.

As mentioned earlier, the LTV covenant is a ratio to measure the loan amount against the property's value. The LTV covenant basically says that the maximum LTV during the life of the loan can't be more than a certain percentage, which is typically the same as the starting LTV. For example, if the maximum LTV initially is 65%, there is usually a maximum LTV covenant of 65% during the life of the loan. If the LTV rises above the LTV covenant, you could be required to come in with cash to pay down the loan (i.e., principal balance reduction) or come up with an alternative solution (such as pledging additional collateral on the loan) to bring the loan back into compliance with the covenant. How can this be you ask? Well, historically, CRE values were always thought to increase, which would naturally lower the LTV over time, not to mention you continuously pay down your principal balance with each payment, which further reduces your LTV. However, during times like the Great Recession this wasn't the case as CRE values actually declined, which resulted in increased LTVs. In turn, banks during this time required borrowers to come in with cash to pay down the principal balance on their loan to get their LTV covenants in compliance.

EXAMPLE 4—
LTV COVENANT CALCULATION

Let's say you have a maximum LTV covenant of 65% and two possible future scenarios (Future Scenario A and Future Scenario B) as shown below.

	Loan Commencement	Future Scenario A	Future Scenario B
Loan Amount	$1,000,000	$950,000	$950,000
CRE Value	$1,600,000	$1,700,000	$1,200,000
LTV	63%	56%	79%

At Loan Commencement, you have an LTV of 63% ($1,000,000/$1,600,000 = 63%).

In Future Scenario A, you pay down the loan balance to $950,000 over a few years, and, at the same time, the value of your property increases to $1,700,000. In this case, your LTV would be 56% ($950,000/$1,700,000 = 56%), and you are in compliance with your LTV covenant since it is less than the max 65% allowed.

In Future Scenario B, you pay down the loan balance to $950,000 over a few years, and, at the same time, the value of your property decreases to $1,200,000. In this case, your LTV would be 79% ($950,000/$1,200,000 = 79%), and you are not in compliance with your LTV covenant because it is greater than the max 65% allowed. In this case, your bank could require you to make a principal reduction of $170,000 so the LTV covenant would be in compliance ($950,000 - $170,000 = $780,000/$1,200,000 = 65%).

Note: Discussions with the bank should take place if you are not in compliance with your loan covenants. If you are not in compliance with your loan covenant due to a one-time, non-recurring event, the bank may consider waiving the loan covenant for that time period. On the other hand, if it is a recurring problem, you need to take steps to resolve it, so work with your bank to figure out what steps need to be taken. Remember, if you are not in compliance with your loan covenants, banks can put the loan in default. A default can increase your interest, fees, and ultimately lead to foreclosure of the property. Needless to say, this can be costly for the borrower and the bank, so it is not beneficial for either party to get to this point.

Amortization

Amortization is basically the time it would take to pay the loan off in full (assuming the loan payment is the same payment each month and paid basically on the same day each month). This is not to be confused with the loan term. If you recall, a typical CRE loan has a term of 10 years (i.e., matures in 10 years), but a 20- to 25-year amortization. If the amortization matched the loan term (10-year amortization), the loan would be paid off in 10 years; however, the monthly loan payment would be *much* larger than a loan with a 25-year amortization. This in turn affects the DSCR, which is why borrowers typically like a longer amortization (not to mention it frees up additional cash flow for borrowers).

EXAMPLE 5—
AMORTIZATION COMPARISON

Let's say you have a property with an NOI of $107,250 and you have a $1,000,000 loan at 6% with 2 options for amortization as shown below.

	Option A 25-Year Amortization	Option B 10-Year Amortization
Gross Rents	$165,000	$165,000
Expenses	($57,750)	($57,750)
NOI	$107,250	$107,250
Loan Payments	$77,316	$133,224
DSCR	1.39	.81

*Numbers above are annualized.

In Option A (25-Year Amortization), you have a DSCR of 1.39, which appears worthy of a loan. This option would provide you with free cash flow of $29,934/year ($107,250 - $77,316 = $29,934), or $2,495/month ($29,934/12 = $2,495).

In Option B (10-Year Amortization), you have a DSCR of .81, which does not appear worthy of a loan. This option would provide you with no free cash flow, it is actually negative cash flow of $25,974/year ($107,250 - $133,224 = - $25,974), or a loss of $2,165/month (-$25,974/12 = -$2,165). This means the property cash flow (NOI) doesn't support the loan payment, which banks don't like, and will likely not lend on because it would not meet the required DSCR. A bank may, however, offer you a longer amortization period in this instance to make the loan work.

Note: The shorter the amortization, the higher the payment; the longer the amortization, the lower the payment (all other things being equal of course).

INDUSTRY STANDARD #8:

Amortization periods are usually 20-25 years.

8

Financing: 3 Primary Drivers

There are 3 *primary* drivers, or 3 primary areas, that banks look at to determine if a loan is feasible and how large of a loan can be given/supported. In turn, this affects the loan structure and thus the loan's rate, term, fees, etc. The 3 primary drivers are: cash flow (i.e., DSCR), LTV/LTC, and borrower(s)/guarantor(s) strength.

Cash Flow (DSCR)

Banks are cash flow lenders; this means that the most important piece of the puzzle is a property's cash flow because this is the primary source of repayment. Banks don't want to foreclose on (take back) a property and spend all the time, labor, and money on the foreclosure process, it is too costly. Banks just want the loan they extended to be repaid (on time) and that comes from the property's cash flow. Banks primarily look at two types of cash flow, or more precisely, two types of DSCRs:

- The subject property's DSCR

- Global DSCR

The subject property's DSCR has already been covered[39] and basically relies on just the property itself. If you recall, the subject property's DSCR = NOI/ Loan Payments.

Global DSCR is really used when there is less reliance on the subject property's cash flow (for example, when you don't just have 3rd party rents, as in an investment property) and the bank needs to rely on other outside cash flow[40]. A good example of this is an owner occupied property. For example, you are an insurance agent and want to buy an office property for your agency and hold the property in an LLC. As the owner of both the LLC and the insurance agency, you can lease the property (essentially to yourself) at any rate you wish (lower than market rents, at market rents, or higher than market rents), you can pay your own salary at any rate you wish, and you can make distributions to yourself as you wish. Although it is likely that you will pay some form of rent from your insurance agency to the LLC and the insurance agency will pay some form of an owner's salary, the real driver of the cash flow at the end of the day is the insurance agency. So, in this case, the bank will look at global cash flow, or the Global DSCR. The bank will take the NOI (or EBIDA) of the LLC less distributions[41], plus the EBIDA of the insurance agency less distributions[42], plus your (the owner's) discretionary cash flow[43] and divide this by the loan payments of the property (and any other debts of the LLC), any **debt service obligations** (loan

---

39 The subject property's DSCR is basically the DSCR that we covered in the prior DSCR section (See Chapter 7).
40 There are many definitions for outside cash flow, but for our purposes, it is any cash flow (income) that is not derived from the subject property.
41 Distributions are paid to owners of the LLC.
42 Distributions are paid to owners of the insurance agency. This, of course, assumes the insurance company is an LLC, Partnership, or S Corporation, otherwise, it would be a dividend (for a C Corporation), rather than a distribution.
43 Officer's discretionary cash flow calculations vary, but in general, it is your net income less estimated living expenses. Living expenses include: power, water, cable, internet, food, gas, etc., and, in general, they are estimated at $25,000 -$50,000 annually, although, in some cases its more and other cases its less. Note: These expenses are items that generally are not listed on your personal credit report.

payments) of the insurance company,[44] and your (the owner's) personal debt service obligations.[45] So, in equation form for this case:

Global DSCR = (subject property LLC's NOI - distributions + insurance agency's EBIDA - distributions + owner's Discretionary Cash Flow)/(subject property LLC's loan payments + insurance agency's debt service obligations + the owner's personal debt service obligations)[46]

In general equation terms, it would look like this:

$$\text{Global DSCR} = \frac{\left(\begin{array}{c} \text{Subject Property's EBIDA} - \text{Subject Property's Distributions} \\ + \text{Operating Company's EBIDA} - \text{Operating Company's Distributions} \\ + \text{Owner's Discretionary Cash Flow} \end{array}\right)}{\left(\begin{array}{c} \text{Subject Property's Debt Service Obligations} \\ + \text{Operating Company's Debt Service Obligations} \\ + \text{Owner's Personal Debt Service Obligations} \end{array}\right)}$$

---

44 Other debt service obligations include any other loan or lease payments of the business (the insurance company in this case), for example: credit card payments, auto loan payments, equipment payments, etc.

45 Personal debt service obligations include any other loan or lease payments you (the owner) hold personally, for example: mortgage payments, auto payments, credit card payments, student loan payments, etc. Note: These payments are items that generally are listed on your personal credit report.

46 As mentioned before, banks can also use EBITDA (in lieu of EBIDA).

EXAMPLE 6—
GLOBAL DSCR CALCULATION

Let's say you have an LLC that holds title to your property that is occupied 100% by your insurance business and the LLC collects rents from your insurance company. Further, you have the following cash flow and debt service obligations:

Global Cash Flow	Annual
Subject Property (LLC's) NOI	$100,000
Less: LLC Distributions	($80,000)
Plus: Insurance Company's EBIDA	$100,000
Less: Insurance Company Distributions	(100,000)
Plus: Owner's Discretionary Cash Flow	$205,000
Total Cash Flow	$225,000
Subject Property Loan Payments	$78,000
Insurance Company Debt Service Obligations	$12,000
Owner's Debt Service Obligations	$50,000
Total Debt Service Requirements	$140,000
Margin	$85,000
Global DSCR	1.61

INDUSTRY STANDARD #9:

Banks like to see the 3 most recent years of financials (tax returns, profit & loss statements, etc.) to see what the cash flow trend is, however, they may accept the most recent 1-2 years of financials in some instances. Remember, OO properties generally require a minimum DSCR of 1.20-1.25 and NOO properties generally require a minimum DSCR of 1.25-1.35.

It is worth discussing **pro forma cash flow**. This is basically just projected or estimated cash flow on a property. It is also worth noting that banks do not like this as much as actual historical cash flow—this is another thing that burned them and got them into trouble during the Great Recession (bank auditors, in turn, don't like it either). Banks usually will not use, or even entertain, this speculated cash flow because it is higher risk (i.e., unproven), however, they may use it in some instances (for example, with multifamily properties), but would likely discount the pro forma cash flow significantly (or at least a good amount) to feel comfortable with it. For example, you have a building that is 50% leased and 50% vacant. You have historical cash flow on 50% of the building (that is leased), and you think you can get 30% more of the building leased in the next 90 days (which would make it 80% leased, leaving only 20% vacant). The bank will likely not rely on 80% (50% leased + 30% projected) of the building being leased to determine cash flow, they will typically rely on just the existing 50% that is leased. Until the tenants are paying rent, it is not real, it is just projected.[47] That being said, if you get a fully executed (i.e., signed) lease for the 30%, and the bank is comfortable with the quality of the tenant, the bank may rely on this cash flow because it is no longer projected cash flow since it is a source of cash flow backed by a legally binding contract (i.e., the lease).

LTV/LTC

Loan-to-Value (LTV) and Loan-to-Cost (LTC) were discussed before,[48] but as a refresher, they are:

LTV = Loan Amount/Value of the Property

LTC = Loan Amount/Cost of the Property

---

47 Note: One other option may be to utilize a variation of global cash flow (i.e., utilize the owner's discretionary cash flow in conjunction with the cash flow from the 50% that is leased), until the remaining vacant space of the building is leased.
48 See Chapter 7.

Banks rely on these ratios to determine the maximum loan amount they will give to a borrower. The LTV will tell a bank how much equity a borrower has in the property, and the LTC will tell them how much cash (or "skin in the game") a borrower has in a property. In theory, these ratios would be identical, but due to various market conditions and cycles, they often do not. That being said, the maximum LTV and maximum LTC a bank will allow is usually about the same (i.e., maximum 75% LTV and maximum 75% LTC).[49] For example, let's say you paid $1,100,000 for a property and it has a value of $1,000,000 and the maximum LTV and LTC for the bank is 75%, you would have the following limits for your loan:

- LTV = $750,000 ($750,000/$1,000,000 = 75%)

- LTC = $825,000 ($825,000/$1,100,000 = 75%)

In this instance, the bank will take the lesser of the two amounts, or $750,000, which is the maximum loan amount they are willing to give.

INDUSTRY STANDARD #10:

Remember, maximum LTV/LTC for OO properties = 75%-80%; maximum LTV/LTC for NOO properties = 65%-70%.

Guarantor Strength

Guarantors have been mentioned before,[50] but a guarantor's strength is derived from a variety of factors, and many are quite subjective. For us, we will focus on a few key factors that are really the main areas of what a bank looks at. From a bank's point of view, it is good to be strong in all of the

---

49 As mentioned before, some will allow a higher LTC maximum, in the neighborhood of 5%-10% higher (for example, if the maximum LTV is 75%, the maximum LTC could be 80%-85%).
50 See Chapter 7.

following areas, however, if a guarantor is weak in one area, they may make up for it by being strong in other areas.

Key Factors:

- **Credit**—this is the personal credit of individual guarantors, which is obtained from the three main credit bureaus: Experian, Equifax, and Transunion (or at least one of these). The credit report that is obtained tells the bank your past payment history including your: credit score, satisfactory accounts, delinquent accounts, and public records, among others. Banks' policies and guidelines vary for what is acceptable credit and what is not. *Banks like to see good credit, and the higher the credit score, the better.*

  - Business credit—this is also frequently obtained for any entity (non-individual) guarantors. It comes from a variety of sources (such as Experian, Paynet, and Dunn & Bradstreet), and also tells the bank about past payment history for a given entity.

- **Net Worth**—this is just an individual's (or entity's) overall strength and is calculated as:

Net Worth = Assets - Liabilities

However, not all net worth's are created equal, even if two individuals have the same numerical net worth. For example, John and Jane both have net worth's of $100,000 as follows:

	Assets	Liabilities	Net Worth
John	$100,000	$0	$100,000
Jane	$5,100,000	$5,000,000	$100,000

John, in many cases, would be seen as a stronger guarantor than Jane since he has zero liabilities (debts) and Jane has liabilities of $5,000,000. When times get tough, John has no debt obligations to pay, while Jane has debt obligations related to the $5,000,000 to pay. *Banks like to see a strong net worth, and the higher the net worth, the better.*

- **Liquidity**—this is included in a guarantor's Net Worth and are comprised of assets that are liquid. **Liquid assets** are equal to cash or assets that can be converted to cash quickly (i.e., almost immediately). Some examples of liquid assets include: cash, stocks, bonds, cash value of life insurance, etc. Note: Examples of *non*-**liquid assets** (i.e., fixed assets) include things such as a house or a car, since these items typically can't be converted to cash immediately. *Banks like to see good liquidity, and the higher the liquidity, the better.*

- **Outside Cash Flow**—this was briefly covered in the Global DSCR section; again, it is cash flow outside of the subject property's cash flow (i.e., it is cash flow other than that derived from the subject property). Banks view this as additional strength because it is another source for repayment of the loan that could be used if necessary. For example, let's say Dr. Jones purchased an office building as an investment and the tenants vacated. After the tenants vacated, the property sat vacant for 6 months until a new tenant moved in. During this 6 month gap the property was vacant and thus earning no income (i.e., rents) — who is making the loan payments at this time (especially if there was no cash set aside while the property was earning income)? You guessed it, Dr. Jones that has other income "outside" of the income the property earns. Now you can see why banks like to see some outside cash flow from guarantors. Keep in mind that there are numerous sources of outside cash flow out there, not just wages. *Banks like to see some source of outside cash flow– the higher the outside cash flow, the better.*

- **Contingent Liabilities**—these are other liabilities (or debt) that guarantors have (i.e., they are guarantors on other loans). Banks look at these in a variety of ways, but to keep it short, the amount of contingent liabilities and how leveraged they are is of importance to banks (Remember John and Jane in the net worth section just mentioned?). To illustrate, let's say a bank has 2 guarantors that are equally strong (same net worth, liquidity, outside cash flow, etc.) and both guarantee a $1,000,000 loan. Further, Guarantor A has $1,000,000 in contingent liabilities and Guarantor B has $20,000,000 in contingent liabilities. Based on guarantors with what appears to be the same strength, Guarantor B is inherently a riskier bet since they have more debt and thus more obligations to pay. If everything went downhill, Guarantor B would likely be more cash flow stressed than Guarantor A. Now, let's say Guarantor A has leveraged their contingent liabilities to 75% (i.e., their other properties have an LTV of 75%, which means they only have 25% equity in them), but Guarantor B has leveraged their contingent liabilities to 40% (i.e., their other properties have an LTV of 40%, which means that they have 60% equity in them), now it looks different right? Guarantor B looks a lot stronger now due to the lower leverage. *Banks like to see few contingent liabilities, and the fewer the contingent liabilities, the better.*

- **Character**—this one is definitely subjective and undefined. You establish character primarily through existing relationships with banks, although sometimes a story of what you have done and have been through can suffice. It is really a judgment call on the bank's part and it used to be given more weight in the past than it does today. Character does still matter however, because when times get tough, it tells the bank if you will stand tall and face the music (i.e., make the loan payments or do everything you can to work with the bank to try to make good on the loan). *Banks like to see a history of good character.*

As you can see from just the few factors and scenarios mentioned, there can be countless pieces to the guarantor puzzle that a bank can put together.

9

What to Expect

I have heard countless times over the years that "this loan is a cookie cutter loan," or "this loan is simple and straight forward." While those statements may have been true 20 or even 10 years ago, it is almost never true now. There are just simply no "cookie cutter" or "simple" loans anymore. Every loan now has *some* hair on it (or a lot of hair on it), and more likely than not, some hurdle(s) to get over.

That being said, it varies on what to expect from loan to loan, because each CRE loan is unique. There are, however, some general steps when applying for a loan, and we will go through them here. Keep in mind that several of these steps can be skipped or combined into one. For example, you may have your initial meeting (Step 1), discuss terms with your bank verbally (skipping Steps 2-4), and provide them a full (or nearly complete) package to begin their formal underwriting immediately (Step 5). So, without further ado, here they are:

General Steps:

1. Initial Meeting—meet with the bank/lender to discuss what you are looking to do (i.e., purchase/refinance a property, overview of the property, general loan terms/structure/fees (at least in the ballpark), loan requirements, timing to close, etc.).

2. Preliminary Package—submit a preliminary package to the bank to allow them to determine if what you are requesting is feasible and within their parameters. The preliminary package can include some or all of the following on the property and guarantors: purchase agreement (if buying), existing loan statement (if refinancing), rent roll, leases, property tax returns, property profit & loss statements, operating company tax returns (if OO), operating company profit & loss statements (if OO), and guarantor's financials (tax returns, personal financial statement, etc.), among others.

3. **Term Sheet (aka Letter of Interest)**—after the bank has reviewed the preliminary package, and the loan request appears doable (that's a technical term), the bank will then extend you a Term Sheet. This Term Sheet or Letter of Interest (**LOI**) will go over the *proposed* financing and general structure of what they can offer you. It will discuss the general terms such as: the borrower, the guarantors, the loan amount, the term, the amortization, the interest rate, the fees, etc. Note: It is important to note that the Term Sheet is *not* a commitment (as many borrowers think that it is), it is just an expression of interest to do the loan. However, the Term Sheet is usually very similar, if not exact, on what will ultimately be reflected in the commitment letter (to be discussed shortly).

4. When you, the borrower, accept the terms of the Term Sheet, you sign it and return it to the bank, along with (in many cases) a deposit. By signing the term sheet, it basically just acknowledges that you agree to the terms the bank is proposing. (If you don't accept the terms of the Term Sheet, it goes no further, and the process stops.) Remember, the bank is going to put in a lot of time and labor into the loan (and you will be putting in some time in the form of providing information), so it is best that everyone be on the same page from the get go so no one is spinning their wheels, hence the reason for the Term Sheet.

5. Once the Term Sheet is accepted, the bank will request additional information from you (to make it a complete loan package) and will begin the formal underwriting process. During the underwriting process, additional information is almost always needed because things arise (or are uncovered) throughout the process. This may be easier said than done, but some good advice during this process is to *be patient.*

6. Once the loan is underwritten, the bank submits it for approval, and, upon approval, the bank will issue you a **Commitment Letter** on the general loan terms, including those items mentioned in the LOI above, but expanded, and with additional detail. The Commitment Letter is the actual *commitment* to lend, and it usually is a conditional commitment letter which states that certain conditions must be met or done prior to finalizing the loan (along with obtaining and signing loan documents). Some of the common conditions that are typically required prior to loan close include obtaining: an appraisal, an environmental

report, a title policy, insurance, **SNDAs/Estoppels**[51] (if applicable), and verification of liquid assets (i.e., liquidity), if not done already, among others.

7. Once the conditions stated in the Commitment Letter are met, loan documents are ordered, reviewed, revised if needed (sometimes several times depending how many reviewers there are … this goes out to you attorneys), and final documents are completed. The borrower then signs the finalized loan documents, which includes the **Deed of Trust** (or alternatively, a mortgage, depending on what state you are in)[52], and, once the Deed of Trust is recorded[53], you close on your loan. On a side note, after banks went through the Great Recession, most of them only like to take a First Deed of Trust, or 1st lien position, on a property. They don't like to take a Second Deed of Trust, or 2nd lien position, on a property much anymore since they want to have priority in the property if things go downhill in the future.

---

51 SNDA stands for Subordination Non-Disturbance and Attornment and it is an agreement between the borrower, the bank, and a tenant. In a nut shell, this document states that: (1) the tenant's lease is subordinate to the bank's loan (i.e., the bank has a 1st lien position on the property and the loan has priority over the tenant's lease), (2) if the loan goes sideways and the bank takes the property via foreclosure, the bank will honor the lease and not disturb the tenant, and (3) the tenant will attorn to the bank (i.e., the tenant will honor the lease and recognize the bank as the new landlord). The Estoppel, is also an agreement between the borrower, the bank, and a tenant. In a nutshell, this document states that: (1) the tenant's lease is valid, (2) there is no default under the lease, (3) there is no prepaid rent except that which is stated in the lease, and (4) the lease has not been modified or assigned. Note: The SNDA/Estoppel Agreement is often a single document and the execution of this document is very common in the industry since it is a requirement for financing. Further, there is usually an SNDA/Estoppel that needs to be executed by each tenant, so, if you have 10 tenants, there are likely to be 10 SNDAs/Estoppels that need to be executed.
52 The Deed of Trust is a security instrument on the property (i.e., it is a document that gives security interest in the property to the bank until the loan is paid in full) that states who holds title to a property, who the lender is, and what the loan amount is, among other things. It is a legal document that is recorded, so if the loan goes sideways, the lender can foreclose on the property.
53 Recording typically takes place at the county recorder's office. When a document is recorded, it serves as a notice to the world. In this case, it notifies the world (i.e., the public) that a property has been encumbered (i.e., a security interest in the property has been taken) by the bank, and the bank has a loan on the property.

8. Just another thing to mention, again, is to *be patient*. Remember, CRE finance is different than the more cookie-cutter residential real estate finance world (no offense to the residential lenders reading this) and nearly every deal is different (not to mention more complex). A *typical* time range to go through the whole process (assuming the bank has a full package in hand) is 30-60 days, however, this can change depending on any issues uncovered, hurdles to get over, workload of the banker, workload of 3rd parties, and the complexity of the deal.

Timing

Timing to close on a loan can vary dramatically depending on all the variables of the request including: how simple or complex it is, the current workload of the bank at the time of the loan request (Can they start underwriting today, or will it take them two weeks just to start looking at it?), and the current workload of 3rd parties (appraisers, title companies, attorneys, etc.) at the time of the loan request (Can they start today, or is it weeks down the road for them as well?).

Some things banks consider in regards to the simple/complex question include:

- Is it a basic property or unique (special use) property?

  o A simple office property is a lot easier to analyze than a bowling alley or golf course.

- Is there a single tenant or fifty tenants?

  o Reviewing 1 lease is a whole lot easier than reviewing 50 leases.

- Is the ownership structure (and therefore borrowers/guarantors) simple or complex (i.e., how many entities need to be reviewed)?

    o Reviewing 1 **Operating Agreement**[54] is a whole lot easier and less labor intensive than reviewing 10 Operating Agreements.

    o In similar fashion, reviewing 1 entity's financials (tax returns, profit & loss statements, etc.) are a whole lot easier than reviewing 10 entities' financials.

Every borrower/guarantor should consult with their attorney and accountant on how to hold their property, however, the more complex the loan request is, the more time it will take the bank to analyze the loan request. Also, the more complex the loan request, the more it *may* cost you (in terms of fees and/or rate) since it needs to make sense for the bank, after all, they are in business to make money.

Okay, back to timing. Assuming you have a basic to average deal in terms of complexity, and the workload of the bank and 3rd parties are average, it should take roughly 30-60 days to close (once the bank receives the package). Here is a *rough* estimate on what to expect:

---

54 An operating agreement is a governing document for LLCs on how it runs its operations. It lays out what the LLC's purpose is, how it will function, who the members (or owners) are, who the managers are, what decisions can be made by who, what assets it can hold, etc..

*3rd Party Reports typically include the following: appraisal, environmental, and title report. Also, SNDAs/Estoppels can be sent out during this time (most national/credit tenants have a 14-30 day response clause in their lease to get the SNDA/Estoppel back to the landlord).

III

Other Loan Types

Up to this point we have only discussed a typical portfolio term loan, but it would be remiss of me not to at least mention (at least briefly) two other loan types since they are pretty common, and they are:

- Construction Loans

- SBA Loans

As there are varying degrees and varying products of both of these loan types, we will be focusing on the common ones in this section.

10

Construction Loans

Construction Loans are just what they sound like, to construct, or build a building or project (single family residential (SFR) developments can also be thrown in here). Construction Loans are not to be taken lightheartedly—there is more work (and monitoring … and fees … and headache) associated with these types of loans since there is more due diligence on these (compared to a typical portfolio term loan) to ensure that it will be a successful project, not to mention everyone is trying to cover all their bases so they are not liable for anything. Remember, this is the type of loan that took many banks down (i.e., caused bank failures) during the Great Recession.

Some of the things banks (and title companies—they got burned too) have to look at while underwriting constructions loans, *in addition to* those items in a typical portfolio term loan, are:

- the general contractor (resume, license, history with the state contractors board, insurance, and possibly their financials)

- subcontractors (possibly additional information from them)

- material suppliers (possibly additional information from them)

- **cost breakdown(s)**[55]

- plans and specs[56]

- construction contract[57]

- architect's contract[58]

- **voucher control** contract[59]

The above items are by no means exhaustive because it is a pretty basic baseline list, but analyzing these things along with everything else in a term loan is pretty labor intensive. And this is just the start to get the loan closed. After closing, it is an ongoing labor intensive project with all of the disbursements of loan funds as the building is built, and making sure the

---

55 A breakdown of the costs for the construction project, typically broken out line by line (i.e., permits, concrete, framing, plumbing, etc.).

56 The building plans (typically drawn up by an architect) and specifications—how will the building be built (for example, wood siding or stucco, concrete tile roof or asphalt shingle roof, what type of flooring, etc.)

57 A contract between the property owner and the general contractor, which among other things is a contract that spells out the time to build the project, the cost of the project, how changes will be managed, etc.

58 A contract between the property owner and the architect.

59 A contract between the property owner, the general contractor, the bank, and the voucher control company. A voucher control company is often a 3rd party service that monitors the construction project through inspections as the project progresses and manages the disbursement of funds to the contractor/subcontractors. The intent of the voucher control company is to help ensure that everyone is paid out on time, for work completed, on a specified project, as agreed, to avoid any contractor/subcontractor payment disputes that could lead to encumbering the property with liens for work performed, but not paid. Sometimes banks have their own internal voucher control department, or sometimes a bank and a 3rd party voucher control company split duties.

invoices, lien releases[60], and inspections all reconcile (i.e., match up) and are within budget, not to mention having to rework the numbers over and over again with any change orders, and hoping the project is delivered on time … and this is just a glimpse.

Two pieces of wisdom here, sit down with your banker up front to go over their processes in a construction loan, and, DO NOT start *any* construction on the property (this even includes demo work, temporary fencing, parking a tractor on the property, or even pulling weeds!) prior to getting a construction loan, otherwise you may not be able to get one because the bank may not be able to get proper title insurance due to an issue called **broken priority**.[61]

That being said, there are 2 main types of construction loans: **Non-Revolving Lines of Credit (NRLOC)** and **Revolving Guidance Lines.**

Non-Revolving Line of Credit (NRLOC)

An **NRLOC** is typically for a single building (or project) and, as the name implies, it doesn't revolve (i.e., once you borrow the funds, you can't pay the loan down and borrow again). You will typically have additional fees associated with this type of loan including: loan fees, voucher control/

---

60 A Lien Release (lien waiver) is a document that is signed by the contractor, subcontractor, material supplier, or other party that is involved in the construction project that basically says they have been paid for work performed and that they "release" or "waive" any lien rights to the property.

61 Broken priority is when construction begins on a property prior to the construction loan being in place and prior to the deed of trust securing the loan is recorded. If there is broken priority, title companies are hesitant to give the bank the title insurance (and endorsements) they need (i.e., a priority [1st] lien position aka first deed of trust), which could hold up the loan. The reason for the hesitance is that there is potential for an unrecorded lien (mechanic's lien) to be filed/recorded from the contractor (or subcontractor) that performed the work on the property prior to the loan finalizing, in which case, if this happened, it would take precedence over the bank's position. If this were the case, the title company that insured the bank of the 1st lien position could potentially take a loss if the lien is not paid. The couple of options that title may be able to work with to move forward in the event there is broken priority is to get all contracts/invoices/lien releases from contractors for all work performed, or to wait the statutory time period for any potential mechanic's lien to lapse.

inspection fees, and title fees. These loans are typically to the owner of a property (who hires a contractor to build the building), or they are made directly to a contractor/developer, who happens to own the property (land) that they will be building on. These loans can just be for the construction of the building, or they can be construction to permanent loans (i.e., upon completion of construction they convert into a term loan).

Note: Don't expect to get speculative financing with this loan type; rather, it should be used for OO CRE projects or NOO CRE projects that are pre-leased (i.e., leased prior to construction commencement), such as a **build-to-suit** project[62]. Although there may be some banks out there willing to finance spec construction, most won't or prefer not to because they are (or at least seen as) a higher risk. Remember, construction loans are riskier than term loans because the project is not yet built and things can go sideways in a hurry. Speculative financing in general is also risky because the property is not stabilized. So effectively, for spec construction financing, you are asking a bank to do not just a riskier loan, but a riskier-riskier loan.

INDUSTRY STANDARD #11:

12-18 month term (NRLOC period only, i.e., construction period only), WSJ Prime + 1% - 3% (or LIBOR + 3% - 5%), 1%-1.5% loan fee, voucher fee .5%-1% of disbursed funds amount, additional title fees vary, plus all other fees mentioned in the term loan section that are not mentioned here.

---

62 A build-to-suit project is where a contractor/developer builds a building for the person/ business that will occupy it. For example, a dentist wants a new building built for their dental practice, so the contractor/developer builds the building to the dentist's specifications. A few common ways this can be done is: 1) the dentist owns/purchases the property, obtains financing to build the project, and retains ownership of the building upon completion of construction, 2) the contractor owns/purchases the property, obtains financing to build the project, and sells the dentist the building upon completion of construction, or 3) the contractor owns/purchases the property, obtains financing to build the project, the contractor retains ownership of the building and leases the building to the dentist.

Revolving Guidance Line

A **Revolving Guidance Line** on the other hand, does revolve (i.e., it's like a credit card, you can borrow against it, pay it down, then borrow against it again, pay it down again, over and over again until maturity of the loan) and is typically used for multiple buildings, phases of a project, or SFRs (i.e., houses). This type of loan is similar to the NRLOC with the exception that it revolves. For example, this type of loan is commonly used for an SFR developer who is building several homes (let's say in a subdivision). The developer uses the loan funds to build a house, then sells the house, pays down the loan from the sale proceeds, and then uses the loan funds again to build another house (and so on and so forth). Like the NRLOC, there are additional fees associated with this type of loan and are similar to the NRLOC fees. However, you may get hit with some other fees, say, in this example, a per building (or per house) loan fee, as well as additional voucher control/inspection/title fees.

11

SBA Loans

Small Business Administration (SBA) loans have been all the rage in recent memory since they allow for loan terms outside of a typical portfolio term loan because SBA loans are "supported" or guaranteed by the SBA. They allow banks to do things they couldn't or wouldn't be willing to do conventionally (with a portfolio term loan) since the SBA creates a lower risk loan with either a lower LTV for the bank or a guaranteed portion of a loan for the bank. In similar fashion, they allow borrowers to do things they couldn't or wouldn't be willing to do conventionally (with a portfolio term loan) since the SBA creates support for the borrower by allowing for a higher LTV on their loan (i.e., lower down payment for the borrower) and the possibility of a longer fixed rate term (among other things). Although there is more paperwork (okay, work), some additional fees, and maybe some longer prepayment penalties (depending on the SBA loan type), these loans can be a great way to get a loan done for both the bank and the borrower.

That being said, there are 2 main types of SBA loans:

- **SBA 504**

- **SBA 7(a)**

Before continuing on, it should be noted that both of these types of loans do require a lengthier application, a slightly longer process, and some additional fees. It should also be noted that these loans are for OO CRE only[63] since SBA does not allow for NOO CRE loans. Per SBA guidelines, an OO CRE property is defined as a property that is at least 51% occupied by the *owner* of the property and is calculated on a square footage basis.[64] That being said, SBA does consider some funky property types as OO (that would seem on the surface to be NOO), such as self-storage facilities and hotels/motels. In general, though, just think of a traditional OO property as being OO. Now, let's jump into these two main types of SBA loans.

SBA 504

An **SBA 504** loan allows the borrower to come in with as little as 10% down (typically), rather than the 20%-25% required with a conventional portfolio term loan. The smaller down payment (i.e., cash injection) is allowed since this loan is broken into 2 loans: 1) a bank portfolio term loan, and 2) a **CDC**[65] loan guaranteed by the SBA. The general structure is as follows:

---

63 SBA 504 loans do allow for other financing such as equipment, and SBA 7(a) loans do allow for a bit more than that (i.e., equipment, working capital, acquisitions, etc.), but this book is about CRE financing, not other types of financing, so we will focus on the CRE financing.

64 SBA does allow for you to create a legal entity to hold the real estate, and then lease the property to your operating company that is a separate entity (as previously discussed), as long as the ownership of both is substantially the same.

65 A Certified Development Company (CDC) is a non-profit corporation that works with the SBA and the lender (i.e., bank) to provide financing through the SBA 504 loan program. CDCs are basically authorized by the SBA to underwrite, process, and service loans (the SDOT loans referenced above) through the SBA 504 loan program, on behalf of, and for, the SBA. Note: the CDC does not underwrite, process, and service the bank's portion (i.e., FDOT loan, as referenced above) as the bank does their portion themselves. The CDC does their portion only (i.e., SDOT loan, as referenced above), for the SBA.

- 50% bank portfolio term loan—this loan is secured with a first deed of trust (FDOT) on the property. This essentially equates to a 50% LTV for the bank's loan.

- 40% (CDC) SBA loan—this loan is secured with a second deed of trust (SDOT) on the property. This essentially equates to a 90% combined loan-to-value (CLTV) for the CDC/SBA.

- 10% borrower cash injection—10% down payment from the borrower.

EXAMPLE 7—
SBA 504 LOAN

Let's say you want to purchase a property for $1,000,000 utilizing the SBA 504 loan product. The cash injection (down payment) required would be $100,000 and broken down as follows:

	$	%	LTV
Purchase Price	$1,000,000		
Bank Loan	$500,000	50%	50%
CDC/SBA Loan	$400,000	40%	90%
Borrower Cash Injection	$100,000	10%	

Remember, because the bank provides 50% of the loan and has an FDOT, it is essentially secured with a 50% LTV ($500,000/$1,000,000 = 50%).

The SBA portion on the other hand has an SDOT (i.e., behind the bank's FDOT) and is essentially secured with a 90% CLTV (($500,000 + $400,000)/$1,000,000 = 90%).

The above is a simple example and excludes any loan fees, SBA fees, etc. Note, however, that you may finance some of these fees, which effectively increases your LTV greater than 90%.

As can be seen above, if a bank has a 50% LTV on a property, it is facing less risk since it can sell the property quickly (i.e., at a discount) in the event of default/foreclosure and likely be made whole on its loan. That being said, a bank still needs to underwrite the loan and approve it, as does the CDC. A good rule of thumb is that if a bank is willing to approve the loan while following SBA guidelines, a CDC will be as well, but not so much vice versa.

What will the loan terms be on this type of loan? The *bank portfolio term loan* (or 50% portion) of the SBA 504 loan will have similar terms as the bank portfolio term loan discussed in Section II—Commercial Real Estate Loans. The *CDC/SBA loan* (or 40% portion), however, is a little bit different. The main differences for the CDC/SBA loan are: the term/amortization period, the fixed rate period, and the prepayment penalty. So, here are the differences in slightly more detail:

- The term *and* amortization period are for 20-25 years[66]. So the term is *longer* than a bank's typical 10-year term, and the amortization period can be the same as a bank's typical 25-year amortization period. Remember, the shorter the amortization, the higher the payment, but also, the quicker the loan payoff.

- The fixed rate period is for 20-25 years.[67] That's right, you get a fixed rate for 20-25 years! (Pretty fantastic, right?)

- The prepayment penalty is a declining 10-year penalty: 10, 9, 8, 7, 6, 5, 4, 3, 2, 1. This penalty, however, is calculated a bit different than the bank's portfolio term loan prepayment penalty as discussed in Section II. For instance, it *is not* 10% of the CDC/SBA loan balance the first year. Rather, this penalty is calculated as a percentage of one year's worth of interest on this loan[68], which starts out at 100% of the interest in year 1 and declines 10% per year after that. So, if you paid off the loan in year 1, you would owe a full year's worth of interest as the prepay. If you paid

---

66 The 20-year term/amortization option was typical historically speaking; however, the 25-year term/amortization option has become available as of 2018. In addition, 10-year maturities are also available.
67 Similar to the 25-year term/amortization option becoming available in 2018, the 25-year fixed rate also became available in 2018, albeit at a slightly higher rate than the 20-year option (for the additional 5 years).
68 The interest to calculate the prepayment penalty is not the actual interest rate on the loan as most people know it, it is actually the debenture rate (which is a completely different topic). Just note, the debenture rate is less than the loan rate, so if you calculate the payoff with the actual loan rate, the actual prepayment penalty should be lower than that.

the loan off in year 2, you would owe 90% of one year's worth of interest as the prepay. If you paid the loan off in year 3, you would owe 80% of one year's worth of interest as the prepay. This continues through year 10, where after year 10, there is no prepay.

INDUSTRY STANDARD #12:

10% down payment (i.e., cash injection into the property)

Bank Loan (50% portion)—same terms as described in the portfolio term loan section, but the Loan Fee may increase to 1.5%.

CDC/SBA Loan (40% portion)—As noted above: term = 20-25 years, amortization = 20-25 years, and prepayment penalty = 10 years. The rate will be fixed at time of close (for 20-25 years) and is the going (current) market rate, this is non-negotiable[69]. Fees: various—check out sba. gov to get the latest fees. Note: Many of these fees can be financed in the loan. Also of note, the maximum loan amount for the CDC/SBA loan is $5,000,000[70].

SBA 7(a)

Similar to an SBA 504 loan, an **SBA 7(a)** loan allows the borrower to come in with as little as 10% down (typically), rather than the 20%-25% with a conventional portfolio term loan. An SBA 7(a) loan is different than an SBA 504 loan as the SBA *guarantees* a portion of the SBA 7(a) loan. Historically,

---

69 To find out the current market rate to get a better idea, ask your bank or local CDC for recent rates, ask for at least the last couple of months to get some idea of where they are currently and how they have changed recently.

70 The max loan amount typically is $5,000,000; however, in some instances, this can be increased to $5,500,000. However, assuming a CDC/SBA loan of $5,000,000, this means you could have a building that costs $12,500,000: the bank portion could be $6,250,000 (50% portion), the CDC/SBA portion could be $5,000,000 (40% portion), and the borrower cash injection could be $1,250,000 (10% portion), or, $6,250,000 + $5,000,000 + $1,250,000 = $12,500,000.

SBA 7(a) loans were used for everything other than real estate (i.e., business acquisition, business expansion, equipment purchases, working capital, etc.), and still are; however, these loans have recently trended to include real estate. Rather than reducing the risk for a bank via a lower LTV as with the SBA 504 loan, the SBA 7(a) loan offers a guarantee from the SBA (to the bank) of 75%-85%[71] of the loan amount. In other words, it is one bank loan (a CDC is not involved like in the SBA 504 loan), and the SBA guarantees the bank repayment on the majority (75%-85%) of the loan. For example, if you obtain an SBA 7(a) loan of $1,000,000, the SBA guaranteed portion is 75% of this, or $750,000. This means that the bank's actual risk exposure (i.e., unguaranteed portion) is $250,000 ($1,000,000-$750,000 guaranteed portion = $250,000). Because there is collateral associated with this loan as well, the bank's actual exposure is likely to be far less than $250,000. To wrap your head around this one, let's say you had a $1,000,000 SBA 7(a) loan and the bank had to foreclose and take back the property. The bank then sells the property for $750,000, leaving a remaining loan balance of $250,000. Since the SBA guarantees 75% of this, or $187,500 ($250,000 x 75% = 187,500), the bank is only out $62,500 ($250,000 x 25% = $62,500), or far less than the original $250,000 mentioned above. Of course this does not include any other collateral the bank could liquidate and also doesn't include other costs/fees that are incurred related to the foreclosure, such as attorney fees and the like.

---

71 Typically, an 85% guarantee on loan amounts up to $150,000, and a 75% guarantee on loan amounts greater than $150,000.

EXAMPLE 8—
SBA 7(A) LOAN

Let's say you want to purchase a property for $1,000,000 utilizing the SBA 7(a) loan product. The cash injection required would be $100,000 and would be broken down as follows:

	$	%	LTV
Purchase Price	$1,000,000		
SBA 7(a) Loan	$900,000	90%	90%
Borrower Cash Injection	$100,000	10%	10%
Guaranteed Portion (75%)	$675,000		
Unguaranteed Portion (25%)	$225,000		

Remember, the bank provides the entire loan amount of $900,000 and the SBA guarantees 75% of the loan amount, or $675,000 ($900,000 x 75% = $675,000). The bank's total exposure then (i.e., the unguaranteed portion) is $225,000 ($900,000 x 25% = $225,000). In other words, if the loan goes sideways and all collateral that was liquidated was equal to 0 (i.e., had no value), then the bank would be out $225,000 instead of the $900,000 because of the guarantee. It is important to remember, however, that the bank would highly likely be able to sell the property for something, so the $225,000 unguaranteed portion would likely be significantly reduced.

The above is a simple example and excludes any loan fees, SBA fees, etc. Note, however, that you may finance some of these fees, which effectively increases your LTV greater than 90%.

As can be seen above, even though the bank has a 90% LTV on the property, they are facing less risk since they have 75% of the loan amount guaranteed by the SBA. In the event of default/foreclosure and liquidation of collateral, the bank's losses are likely to be minimal compared to the initial loan amount. This being said, a bank still needs to underwrite the loan and approve it, and obtain the guarantee from the SBA. A good rule of thumb is that if a bank is willing to approve the loan and follow SBA guidelines for the guarantee, the SBA will likely provide the guarantee, but not so much vice versa.

So what will the loan terms be on this type of loan? For the most part, the terms will be similar to the bank portfolio term loan with a few notable differences:

- As with the bank portfolio term loan, the amortization period can be 25 years. However, instead of a 10-year term (like on the bank portfolio term loan), the SBA 7(a) term *can* stretch to 25 years.

- The rate will either be a floating (i.e., variable) rate at the Wall Street Journal Prime Rate + 2.25% to 2.75% (this is a typical range, and this rate will adjust quarterly), or the rate will be fixed similar to the bank portfolio term loan discussed in Section II.

- Prepayment penalties can range a little, but the typical prepayment penalty is a 5, 3, 1 prepayment penalty. In other words, if you pay the loan off in year 1, you would have a prepay of 5% of the loan amount. If you paid the loan off in year 2, you would owe 3% of the loan amount. If you paid the loan off in year 3, you would owe 1% of the loan amount; after year 3, there would be no prepayment penalty.

INDUSTRY STANDARD #13:

10% down payment (i.e., cash injection into the property)

Bank Fees—same as described in the portfolio term loan section, but the Loan Fee will instead be a packaging fee of $2,500 or less.

As noted above: term = up to 25 years, amortization = 25 years, and prepayment penalty = 3 years (i.e., a 5, 3, 1 prepayment penalty). The rate will be floating as noted above, or fixed similar to a portfolio term loan (typically fixed for 5 years, and reset every 5 years). Fees: various—check out sba.gov to get the latest fees. Note: Many of the fees can be financed in this loan. Also of note, the maximum loan amount of the SBA 7(a) loan is $5,000,000[72].

On a side note, I suggest that you work with an SBA Preferred Lender if you are going the SBA 7(a) route. A Preferred Lender is a lender that does so many of these loans that they get a "preferred" status that essentially expedites the process because of the lender's knowledge and experience with this type of lending, which is always handy to have if you are the borrower.

A Preferred Lender basically means that once the bank approves the loan, they submit to the SBA for the guarantee and it is usually approved by the SBA (i.e., the SBA usually just rubber stamps it, more or less, assuming the bank follows SBA guidelines). If a bank is *not* a Preferred Lender, the process can often times take longer as the bank submits to the SBA, waits for approval (or word that changes need to be made), makes changes if needed, re-submits, and so-on and so-forth. This back and forth can add weeks, or months, to the process. The real difference between a Preferred Lender and not is really just the volume of SBA 7(a) loans the Preferred Lender does—they do so many that they know the process hands down,

---

72 The max loan amount typically is $5,000,000, resulting in an SBA guarantee amount of $3,750,000 ($5,000,000 x 75% guaranteed portion = $3,750,000).

they know what the SBA is looking for, and they know what flies and what doesn't, and, subsequently, the trust factor from the SBA increases.

"A Final Thought"

Every bank has different appetites for different types of loans and are thus more aggressive with certain types, and less aggressive with other types. This has to do with the bank's loan concentrations, credit risk, interest rate risk, and other factors on the bank's own balance sheet, as well as the overall economy, regulations, and various other factors. In other words, they may be hungry for a certain loan type one day, and not so hungry for that same loan type the next. Also, different banks can do different things (and their appetites are different), so take a look at maybe 2 or 3 banks to see what they can do and how competitive they are for the particular type of loan you are looking for. I would say 2-3 banks is healthy competition, but shopping 10-15 banks is a waste of your time and theirs. Not to mention, if they get wind of it, they may be less inclined to work on your deal, and put less effort in, so it may end up going against you if you shop tons of banks, but 2-3 banks is good and fair.

Another thing to note is that interest rates and terms are not everything. Having a relationship with bankers/lenders can prove more beneficial than a .25% or .50% better rate with someone you don't have a relationship with. In good times, they can provide guidance and creativity to meet your goals, they can understand your goals, and they know you and your business, so it will save you time explaining it over and over again to a new face. In bad times, they may be more willing to work with you, whether with delayed payments or a full blown restructure. So, just think about the value in a banking relationship. I have heard time and time again from my borrowers/clients how much they value our relationship and my opinion, candidacy, creativity, foresight, honesty, and hard work to make their goals and dreams become a reality. In the end, it is about doing my job, doing what's best for the client, and doing what's best for the bank—which, in fewer words, is all about the relationships I have with my clients.

IV Index/Reference

Symbols

D

E

F

G

I

L

M

N

11 Things You Should Ask the Bank (if you are looking for a CRE loan)

1) Are you guys lending on _____ properties currently? (Fill in the blank for the property type—i.e., office, retail, industrial, multifamily, etc.)

2) What is the maximum LTV/LTC you would lend on this property?

3) What is the minimum DSCR you would allow on this property?

4) Where do you think interest rates would be today for this loan? For how long would the interest rate be fixed?

5) How long is the loan term?

6) How long is the amortization period?

7) What are the fees associated with this loan?

8) Would the interest rate, loan term, or fees improve with a lower LTV, greater DSCR, or expanded relationship (i.e., other business such as deposit accounts) with the bank?

9) Is it possible to have non-recourse (no guarantors) on the loan?

10) Assuming you have a full loan package in hand today, what does the timing look like to get this closed?

11) What do you need from me to get the process started? (financials, entity documentation, information on the property, etc.)

Note: Each of these questions will open up discussion and lead to other questions and answers, which will be helpful for both you and the bank.

Another note: If you go over these questions with them, but they don't seem inclined to lend, or, for instance, they aren't lending on a particular property type at the moment, ask if they know another bank/lender who is or might be.

ABOUT THE AUTHOR

John Crefin has more than 15 years of experience in the banking industry, with a specialty in commercial real estate lending. His experience has spanned hundreds of millions of dollars in loans over his career, which includes a wide degree of property types. He has authored and co-authored bank lending policy and bank loan underwriting guidelines.

Mr. Crefin has been an adjunct professor and guest lecturer at universities in the United States and Europe. As a seasoned professional, he has also been a featured speaker and panelist at the occasional CRE forecast. He holds an MBA from the University of Nevada, Reno.